Dublin

The Ultimate Dublin Travel Guide By A Traveler For A Traveler

The Best Travel Tips; Where To Go, What To See And Much More

Table of Contents

Why Lost Travelers Guide

Chapter 1: Welcome to Dublin:

- History
- Geography
- Climate

Chapter 2: Cultural Experiences in Dublin

Chapter 3: Where to Go and What to See

Chapter 4: Transportation Methods within the City

Chapter 5: Where to Eat

Chapter 6: Where to Stay

Chapter 7: Unique Dublin Experiences

Chapter 8: Shopping Destinations

Chapter 9: Nightlife in Dublin

Chapter 10: Safety Tips and Survival Guide

Conclusion

Why Lost Travelers Guides?

First, we want to wish you an amazing time in Dublin when you plan to visit. Also we would like to thank you and congratulate you for downloading our travel guide, *"Dublin; The Ultimate Dublin Travel Guide By A Traveler For A Traveler"*.

Tired of long, boring, and biased guides out in the market that not only waste our time but also waste money? So were we! We continuously had to ask someone for the simplest things that could have easily been found if we could speak the language of the location, or information that should have been in the guide we were using at that time! As we continuously face this problem we decided we should create a guide that that would cover everything a traveler needs to know from the point of Arrival to Departure, and the Lost Travelers Guides were born.

When having our guides created we take a lot into consideration such as time, therefore our guides are short and to the point. But mainly we ask ourselves and other travelers what we enjoy during a travel and what we wish we had known prior to visiting the location and that is where the Lost Travelers guides excels. As the Lost Travelers Guide team, we only have one goal and that is to make sure that our guides are the best out, and provides the most value available.

Each one of our guides are created by a team of professional researchers and travelers whom account every detail about the location from a brief history to amazing travel tips including where to go, what to see and much more. Once our guides have been created we then go over and double check to make sure we are providing our travelers with a fun, engaging, informative and the most powerful travel guide on the market.

"The World Is A Book And Those Who Do Not Travel Only Read One Page"

- St. Augustine

Thanks again for choosing us, we hope you enjoy!

© Copyright 2016 by Seven Tree Group Inc. - All rights reserved.

This document is geared towards providing exact and reliable information in regards to the topic and issue covered. The publication is sold with the idea that the publisher is not required to render accounting, officially permitted, or otherwise, qualified services. If advice is necessary, legal or professional, a practiced individual in the profession should be ordered.

- From a Declaration of Principles which was accepted and approved equally by a Committee of the American Bar Association and a Committee of Publishers and Associations.

In no way is it legal to reproduce, duplicate, or transmit any part of this document in either electronic means or in printed format. Recording of this publication is strictly prohibited and any storage of this document is not allowed unless with written permission from the publisher. All rights reserved.

The information provided herein is stated to be truthful and consistent, in that any liability, in terms of inattention or otherwise, by any usage or abuse of any policies, processes, or directions contained within is the solitary and utter responsibility of the recipient reader. Under no circumstances will any legal responsibility or blame be held against the publisher for any reparation, damages, or monetary loss due to the information herein, either directly or indirectly.

Respective authors own all copyrights not held by the publisher.

The information herein is offered for informational purposes solely, and is universal as so. The presentation of the information is without contract or any type of guarantee assurance.

The trademarks that are used are without any consent, and the publication of the trademark is without permission or backing by the trademark owner. All trademarks and brands within this book are for clarifying purposes only and are the owned by the owners themselves, not affiliated with this document.

Chapter 1 Welcome to Dublin

Home to some of the most talented people in the world such as best-selling boybands *Westlife* and *Boyzone*, rocker Bono, and author Cecelia Ahern, Dublin certainly has a lot to offer. With medieval roots and rustic charm, there is no doubt that there's a lot to see and so much to know while there.

Dublin is the capital city of Ireland. More than that, the *Fair City*, as it is often called, also boats of natural and man-made wonders that not only capture the eye, but would also leave some special memories in your heart. And now, you have the chance to learn more about Dublin—before you go and actually set foot there.

Brief History

Once called *Baile Àtha Cliath* or *Town of the Hurdled Ford,* the Bay of Dublin has been populated by people since prehistoric times, and was said to have settled as a city in 988 AD. *Dublin* was coined from *Dublind*, a Gaelic word that means black pool, a reference to the River Poddle, which is known as a dark tidal pool located near the Dublin Castle's Gardens in Liffey.

Back in the 10th century, a Scandinavian Viking Settlement was established in the city of Dublin. Up until the Norman Invasion of Ireland in 1169, the Vikings were known to have control of the city. After getting hold of Dublin, the Earl of Pembroke, Strongbow, then declared himself the King of Leinster, prompting King Henry II of England to invade the city and call himself its King in 1171, establishing Dublin as a county together with other liberties before Dublin was separated from the barony in 1840.

In 1204, the Dublin Castle was established as the center of Irish Power, and Dublin became one of the most popular medieval cities in the world. When the infamous Black Death happened in 1348, thousands of original Dubliners were killed, but eventually, good things happened to the city, such as being incorporated as *Pale* in the English Crown.

In the 16th century, England's Queen Elizabeth I established Trinity College as a sign that she wanted Dublin to be Protestant, too. In the 1700s, and with the help of the linen and wool trade, Dublin once again surged—even reaching a population of 50,000!

For a while in the Georgian Times of the 18th Century, Dublin was recognized as the fifth largest city in Europe with the Custom House and the Four Courts among the most notable architecture as their medieval façade was not affected by the changing of the times. Lots of buildings and districts—including the Royal Exchange, the Parliament House, and the Merrion Square, among others, were also built during the 18th century, helping the city's rise as one of the most beautiful places in Ireland, and in the whole of Europe.

Dublin was mostly destroyed after the Irish War of Independence in 1916, but thanks to the help of the Government of the Irish Free State, the city, together with its parliament, was rebuilt, and has continually grown—up until today.

Geography

Located at the Liffey River's mouth, Dublin is small—but definitely packed in its 44 sq mi of area. The north and west both have flat farmlands, while the south is bound by low mountain ranges. Liffey is also responsible for dividing Dublin into two main areas, while other rivers, namely Royal Canal, Grand Central, River Dodder, and River Tolka all run towards the Dublin Bay, covering certain parts of the city with water, and keeping climate cool and steady.

The Southern Part of Dublin is known to house middle to upper class residents, houses, and establishments, while the Northern Part is said to be for the working class—showing differences in architecture and suburbs, as well.

Climate

Dublin has a maritime climate—which means there's a lack of extreme temperatures, and that you could enjoy mild winters and cool summers the rest of the year. May and June are known to be the sunniest months, while October is the wettest with 76mm of rain, on average.

Dublin is also known to be the driest place in Ireland because of its location. Maximum temperature in July is 20.2 C, while January temperature could drop to 8.8 C.

Best Time to Visit

It's best to visit Dublin when the weather is sunny—or during the months of May and June. However, if you want cheaper flight or accommodation rates, you might as well go during the winter months, but make sure to wear warm clothing, as it could get really cold.

Chapter 2 Cultural Experiences in Dublin

One of the best things about Dublin is that it is rich in culture and history. Dublin also offers cultural immersion experiences, where you can try the best that the city has to offer, while learning about its history, too.

Whether it's about spending time at a pub, eating the Irish traditional breakfast (a plate with *sausage, eggs, bacon, black pudding, half a tomato, hashbrowns,* and *baked beans*), playing *trad music,* or watching football, you can try them all in Dublin—and you can start with the ones listed below...

Dublin Traditional Irish Music Pub Crawl

($14.75 and up)

Duration: approx 2 hrs 30 mins

Departure Point: Temple Bar, Dublin

Departure Time: 7:15 PM

With this fun pub crawl, you will be able to experience Dublin's Irish music and pub scene—while being toured by two of the friendliest musicians around. Apart from pub crawls at *The Palace Bar, the Legal Eagle,* and *Isodes Tower,* among others, you'd also be able to listen to traditional Irish stories and songs, and impressive commentary about why these stories and songs are important to Dublin culture.

Bookings: http://www.viator.com/tours/Dublin/Dublin-Traditional-Irish-Music-Pub-Crawl/d503-2932MPC

Traditional Irish House Party and Dinner Show

($22.69 and up)

Duration: approx 3 hours

Departure Point: The Irish House Party Pub and Restaurant

Departure Time: 6:45 PM for dinner and show | 8:30 for show alone

Imagine being able to party—in the traditional Irish way! With storytelling, diverse music and traditional food such as Bailey's infused chocolate cake, you'll have fun spending time with locals and fellow tourists alike. You can also choose if you want the traditional three-course Irish dinner alone, or if you want to experience both the dinner and the show.

Bookings: http://www.viator.com/tours/Dublin/Dublin-Traditional-Irish-House-Party-including-Dinner-and-Show/d503-2886PARTY

Glengalough and Kilkenny City Day Trip

($37.44 and up)

Duration: approx 9 hrs 30 mins

Departure Point: Gresham Hotel 8:10 AM | Gardiner Street Townhouse Guesthouse 8 AM | College Green Ulster Bank 8:20 AM | Jury's Hotel Christchurch 8:30 AM

Departure Time: 8 to 8:30 AM (as listed above)

If you want to spend the day visiting nearby medieval castles that will literally make you feel like you have gone back in time, you'd enjoy this day trip of some of Ireland's most popular castles and old towns.

Apart from the Kilkenny Castle, you'd also be able to visit Glengalough's Medieval Monastic Settlement via luxury coach while learning about Ireland's history.

Bookings: http://www.viator.com/tours/Dublin/Kilkenny-City-and-Glendalough-Day-Trip-from-Dublin/d503-5300CASTLES

Cliffs of Moher (with Galway City and Atlantic Way) Day Tour

($56.72 and up)

Duration: approx 13 hours

Departure Point: City Center or local Dublin hotel (to be discussed)

Departure Time: 7 AM

Balk away from the city center and visit the ruins of the old town of Moher. This Cliffside settlement has the full cosmopolitan and rustic charm of the old city of Galway—now complete with a state of the art visitor center. While there, you'd also be able to travel along the scenic coastal Atlantic Way—and appreciate Dublin, and all of Ireland even more.

Bookings: http://www.viator.com/tours/Dublin/Cliffs-of-Moher-Tour-Including-Wild-Atlantic-Way-and-Galway-City-from-Dublin/d503-5300MOHER

Old Jameson Distillery Whiskey Tour

($18.15 and up)

Duration: approx 60 minutes

Departure Point: Old Jameson Distillery, Dublin

Departure Time: (to be discussed)

And of course, your cultural immersion would not be complete without joining the Old Jameson Distillery Whiskey Tour. Learn about Old Jameson, the whiskey brand, through a guided tour of the distillery—together with the history of its founder, John Jameson. While there, you'd also be able to compare various tastes of whiskey and even get a complementary *Ginger and Lime* from the bar.

Bookings: http://www.viator.com/tours/Dublin/Old-Jameson-Distillery-Whiskey-Tour-in-Dublin/d503-6818OJDDUB15

Chapter 3 Where to Go and What to See

Now that you have learned more about Dublin, it's time to know where to go next. So, where to go and what to see in Dublin? Here are you answers!

The Guinness Storehouse

St James Gate | +353 14084800

www.guinness-storehouse.com

guinnessstorehouse@guinness.com

Yes, it's the home of that world-famous beer! Around since 1759, the home was leased for 9,000 years, and then came the development of the famous beer—first fermented in the same storehouse.

By visiting, you'll learn exactly what goes on in each pint of beer, and you will also see the giant pint which can store 14.3 million small pints of beer—and eat delectable Irish food, too.

Chester Beatty Library

Clock Tower Building, Dublin Castle, Dublin 2 | 353 14070750

www.cbl.ie/

Open: 10 AM to 5 PM

Not only is the Chester Beatty Library the best library in Ireland, it's also known to be one of the best in the whole of Europe!

Once winning the much-coveted *European Museum of the Year* award, the library will help you cultivate your mind by showing you books and collections from Europe, Asia, North America, and even the Middle East—helping you learn about religions and cultures from all over the world.

Dublin Zoo

Phoenix Park Conyngham Rd Dublin 8| +353 14748900

http://www.dublinzoo.ie

Open: 9:30 AM to 6 PM

The best family attraction in Dublin, the zoo is home to over 600 animals in a well-nurtured setting. There are various areas to see, such as: the Gorilla Rainforest; the African Savanna that houses zebras, rhinos, and giraffes; the Asian Forest and its macaques and Sumatran tigers, and the Kaziranga Forest that houses Asian Elephants. As a registered zoo, Dublin Zoo is amazing because it breeds right, conserves well, and also helps visitors learn how to take care of animals, and why it is important to keep them safe. After visiting, you'd have a better appreciation for animals, that's for sure!

Phoenix Park

Parkgate Street Conyngham Rd Dublin 8 | 353 16770095

http://www.phoenixpark.ie

Located near Dublin Zoo, Phoenix Park is often dubbed as the lungs of Dublin. Rich in lush vegetation and fresh air—together with magnificent trees and trails, you'd certainly feel one with nature while visiting! It's a good place to stay away from the hustle and bustle of the city—and spend your time not just with plants, but with animals, such as deer, too!

National Aquatic Centre

Snugburough Rd, Blanchardstown, Dublin | 353 16464300

www.aquazone.ie | sales@nac.ie

One of the best and most exciting attractions around, the National Aquatic Centre houses the biggest swimming pool in Ireland, and the only diving tank in the country, as well.

There are amazing features you could try, too. Examples include the water roller coaster that is the Master Blaster, the Green Giant Flume slide, the Pirate Ship, and the Flow Rider. Both adults and children would enjoy this.

National Botanic Garden

Botanic Rd, Glasnevin, Dublin | 353 18377596

http://www.botanicgardens.ie

Have an incredible, serene time being surrounded by flowers of every kind at Dublin's very own Botanic Garden. While there, you'd also be able to see majestic herons and swans, and learn about the garden's efforts for conservation—with the help of audio and garden tours. See ¾ million dried plant specimens at the National Herbarium, and visit the DNA Research Lab, as well.

Picnic tables both for people and dogs, fishing equipment, and bicycles are also available—and the best part is that they're open every day before Christmas, and that entrance is absolutely free!

River Liffey

Dublin Docklands Development Authority, Custom House Quay, Docklands, Dublin 1 | 353 18183300

A trip to Dublin wouldn't be complete without visiting the River Liffey—the reason why Dublin is around, in the first place. Pay homage to the majestic river by visiting, and don't forget to take pictures! Blessington Street Basin

Philsborough, Dublin 7 | 353 16057700

Legend has it that the Blessington Street Basin used to be home for faeries and other mythical creatures. With its mystical, medieval charm, it's actually not hard to believe. By visiting, you'd get to see majestic birds in flight, trees of every kind, and a canal that flows to the Owel Lough. Visit and you'd have a good time just relaxing and feeling the calmness of the air. The National Museum of Ireland

Kildare Street, Dublin | 353 16777444

www.museum.ie | marketing@museum.ie

Open since 1890, Ireland's National Museum has some of the best and most diverse archaeological collections in the world. The *Tara Brooch* and the *Ardagh Chalice*, two of the most important pieces of Ireland's history, could be found right here—among many other relics from the Medieval times.

A new feature of the museum is the Kingship and Sacrifice Exhibition Centers where you'd be able to find bog bodies that have been preserved from the Iron Age! You might also learn more about your ancestors while here. St. Stephen's Green

Top end of Grafton St. Dublin 2 | 353 14757816

www.heritageireland.ie/en/dublin/ststephensgreen

St. Stephen's Garden features lush greens, swans, arcs and everything reminiscent of days gone by. And you know what's special about it? Well, it is the fact that it was immortalized in James Joyce's popular novel *Ulysses*—so it would be like you're literally stepping foot in history. Temple Bar

2-5 Wellington Quay, Temple Bar, Dublin 2 | 353 1730700

www.visit-templebar.com

Nope, this isn't just your usual pub. The Temple Bar is one of the most legendary places in all of Dublin, and now, it has been improved with the help of quirky cafes and the funkiest shops you'll ever be able to set foot on. Never leave Dublin without visiting this place!

Chapter 4 Transportation within the City

Now that you know where to go, it's also essential that you learn how you could go around the city. When it comes to transportation in Dublin, here's what you have to know.

Trains

www.irishrail.ie/home/

One way of traversing Dublin is by riding a train. You can try trains called *DART*, which could help you go around Dublin and nearby areas. Journey starts from Howth and Malahide up north all the way to the southlands of Greystones.

Buses

www.dublinbus.ie/

There are also buses in Dublin, specifically the *Dublin Bus*. By taking the bus, you'll be able to travel around Dublin, as well as its neighboring areas, and enjoy the sights.

Trams

www.luas.ie/routes/

The LUAS Tram service is also available. With its help, you can go around Downtown Dublin, as well as the south and southwest parts of the city between 5:30 AM to 12:30 MN! Routes are as follows:

Sagghart to Tallaght

Sagghat to Belgard

Belgard to Connolly

Tallaght to The Point

Bride's Glen to St. Stephen's Garden

Now that you know how to go around the city, it's time to check out where you could eat—all in the next chapter!

Chapter 5 Where to Eat

Dublin has so much to offer when it comes to food—from budget meals to special recipes, the city has them all! Here's where you can eat the best Irish food! Affordable Restaurants

Paulie's Pizza

58 Upper Grand Canal Street, Dublin 2 | 353 16643658

Located at the corner of the Grand Canal Street's South Lotts Road, Paulie's Pizza offers a mix of Italian and European Cuisine with various pizza choices all based on a Neapolitan recipe. All their pizzas are wood-fired, giving them that authentic flair. Aside from pizza, they also offer classic Italian dishes that are cooked to perfection. You can opt to eat inside, but you could also choose an al fresco seating—complete with canopy and blankets for a completely comfortable dining experience.

Jo'Burger Town

4/5 Castle Market, Dublin 2 | www.joburger.ie

If casual dining is your dining, you would surely appreciate Jo' Burger Town, one of the best burger shacks in all of Dublin! Aside from burgers, you can also enjoy delicious homemade cocktails, spritzers, and jams that are so delicious, you'll surely come back for more! Drinks are also available—and you can enjoy your time there while listening to amazing music, as well.

Bunsen

36 Wexford Street, Dublin 2 | 353 15525408

Another burger joint, but this one is an affordable gourmet burger shack curated by Tom Gleeson. His American-style burgers are made with Aberdeen Angus Beef, gooey cheese and are all fried to a crisp—and served with classic milkshakes. Their burgers stay fresh even when bought to-go, too.

Green Nineteen

19 Camden Street, Lower Dublin, Dublin 2 | 353 14789626

www.green19.ie

A relaxing café-bar at Camden Street, Green Nineteen serves meals so fast—without having the quality compromised! With fresh produce used for all the dishes on the menu, you can expect the best affordable dining experience around here. Make sure to order slow-braised pork belly and chorizo, Mexican Green, and Negroni, as well as lamb tagine. A world of flavors would surely burst in your mouth once you choose to eat here.

Middle Class Restaurants
Chez Max

1 Palace Street, Dublin 2 | 353 16337215

www.chezmax.ie

With a picturesque setting—the restaurant is located just outside the Dublin Castle, after all—this French café offers cheese platters, beef bourguinion, moules frites, salads, and tartines that would give you such a spectacular dining experience like you haven't had before. Try their early bird menu and get two platters of food for just €19—or $21!

The Port House Pintxos

12 Eustace Street, Dublin 2 | 353 16728590

With their famous Basque Pintxos—or tapas in the Northern Spanish version, you'll have a good time feeling like you're in another European country—while in Dublin, of course! What's great about this place is that their servings are huge—so if you'd like to eat with family and friends, you might as well go here. Don't forget to order manchego and patatas bravas, too.

Pablo Picante's

4 Clarendon Market, Dublin

Noted to have the best burrito in Dublin, Pablo Picante's Mexican dishes are sure to leave a spectacular taste in your mouth. Once a small burrito bar, Pablo Picante's is now one of the most popular burrito restaurants in the world. Amazing deals for students are also available—just make sure to ask at the bar!

CrackBird

60 Dame Street, Dublin | 353 16169841

Twitter.com/crackbirddublin

In Dublin, CrackBird is known to have brought fried chicken back in fashion. With soy and garlic or buttermilk chicken choices—that you can get either in whole or half, you'd surely have a good time reminiscing about the good old days while eating here. Homemade lemonade and ginger spritz are also available here—and you'd enjoy the sides, too!

High End Restaurants
Locks Brasserie

1 Windsor Terrace, Dublin 8 | 353 14200555

www.locksbrasserie.com

This hole-in-the-wall restaurant has 1 Michelin Star to its name. What's special is that they offer traditional French cuisine—but with an Irish twist, making it eclectic and truly unforgettable. They also offer ala carte lunches and Vegetarian dishes for those who opt for them. Private rooms are also available—just ask the Maitre'd!

L'Ecrivain

109a Lower Baggot Street, Dublin 2 | 353 16611919

www.lecrivain.com

Another Michelin-starred restaurant, L'Ecrivain offers delectable French dishes that are perfect for solo diners and even families. They also have amazing offers for groups, business meeting, and private dining rooms are available, as well.

Fire Restaurant

Dawson Street, Dublin 2 | 353 16767200

www.mansionhouse.ie

Near the beautiful Mansion House, the Fire Restaurant offers food made from local, organic produce which you can enjoy under vaulted ceilings, and while surrounded by stained glass windows, giving you that majestic, opulent feeling as you eat. Their jumbo prawn starters are famous for being extremely good, and you can choose vegetarian dishes, as well. Their desserts are mouth-watering and delectable, too.

Etto

18 Merrion Row, Dublin 2 | 353 16788772

www.etto.ie

With a Michelin Star, and Bib Gourmand Recognition, this restaurant simply offers the best exquisite food in Dublin. You will enjoy their mouth-watering coute de beef that seriously melts in the mouth, and you'll also enjoy their caper salad, kohlrabi, and smoked egg yolk, as well. Don't forget to try their wine—it's truly divine!

Chapter 6 Where to Stay

Of course, it is also important that you know exactly where you should stay while in Dublin. And guess what? There are hotels for your every need—and for the kind of budget you have. Here are the best hotels for you to stay in. Budget Hotels

Durban Residence B & B Dublin

($86/night)

69 Gardiner Street Lower, Dublin 1 | 353 18364668

www.durbanresidence.com

What's amazing about this hotel is that it's near downtown Dublin—where most of the shops, restaurants, bus stations, and trams are, which means it would be easy for you to go around the city.

Once an 18th century townhouse, you'd have a good night's sleep in this rustic hotel—complete with free breakfast and Wi-Fi access!

Hotel Ibis Dublin

($81/night)

Red Cow Roundabout, Dublin 22 | 353 14641480

www.accorhotels.com/gb/hotel-0595-ibis-dublin/index.shtml

Just 6 minutes away from the Red Cow tram stop, this hotel is also strategically located close to the Guinness Storehouse and the National Museum of Ireland, making it easy for you to take in what Dublin has to offer. If you're a pet lover, you'd also appreciate the fact that the hotel is pet-friendly—only with a minimal surcharge. Wi-Fi access is free, and there's a 24/7 snack and relaxed bar available for your convenience.

Travelodge Dublin City Centre Rathmines Hotel

($111/night)

Rathmines Rd, Dublin 6 | 353 14911402

www.travelodge.ie/hotels/286/Dublin-City-Centre-Rathmines-hotel

A mere 2.2 kilometers away from the famous Dublin Castle, you'll have a relaxed time chilling out at this hotel, and enjoy its beautiful en suite bathrooms, too. Pets are also allowed with minimal surcharge.

Holiday Inn Express Dublin

($105/night)

Northwood Park, North Wood, Dublin 9 | 353 18628866

http://www.hiexpressdublin-airport.com/

Near the Dublin Airport and the Guinness Storehouse, this hotel features spacious, airy rooms, a lobby lounge, a bar, and free buffet breakfast. Some rooms also have pull-out sofas for your convenience.

Middle Class Hotels
Morehampton Townhouse Dublin

($142/night)

78 Morehampton Rd, Dublin 4 | 353 16688866

www.morehamptontownhouse.com/

With picturesque trees in the surroundings and fresh air all around, this Victorian townhouse is near the city centre as well as the National Concert Hall where some of the best events in Dublin are held. You can choose from either Irish or Continental breakfast. Wi-Fi access is free.

Lynams Hotel

($207/night)

63/64 OConnell Street, Dublin 1 | 353 18880856

www.lynamshotel.ie/

With simple, low-key rooms that provide comfort and relaxation, you'll have an amazing time staying in this Georgian townhouse is near most shopping centers, and has some of the best Irish and Italian dishes at the on-site restaurant. Wi-Fi access and free breakfast are available, as well.

Jury's Inn Christchurch Dublin

($195/night)

Christchurch Pl, Dublin 8| 353 14540000

www.jurysinns.com/hotels/dublin/christchurch

With their famous Costa Coffee, you'll surely have an unforgettable time in this hotel—not only by resting, but also by trying out what they have to offer, courtesy of their on-site restaurant and bar. Wi-Fi access is available for free.

The Kildare Street Hotel by the Key Collection

(178/night)

47-49 Kildare St, Dublin 2 | 353 16794643

www.thekeycollection.ie/kildare-street-hotel.html

Set atop one of the liveliest clubs and bars around, the Kildare Street Hotel has been around since 1837 when it was first put up. Near the Temple Bar and the National Museum of Ireland, amongst others, rooms have that chic vibe with monochromatic interiors. Split-level rooms are available, and there's also an on-site nightclub where you could have fun in. Snacks and traditional Irish breakfast are also available.

Luxury Hotels
The Fitzwilliam Hotel Dublin

($274/night)

St Stephen's Green, Dublin 2 | 353 14787000

www.fitzwilliamhoteldublin.com/

Surrounded by lush gardens, and with fresh blooms welcoming you in the room, this hotel has that sleek, modern feel coupled with classic charm—its four-poster beds and balconies would give you the sense of royalty that you're craving for! An intimate bar is also around—and you'd get to taste amazing Irish dishes here, too. Meeting rooms and free Wi-Fi access are also available.

The Morrison, a Double Tree by Hilton Hotel

($275/night)

Ormond Quay Lower, Dublin 1 | 353 18872400

www.doubletree3.hilton.com/en/hotels/ireland/the-morrison-a-doubletree-by-hilton-hotel-DUBTMDI/index.html

With amazing riverfront views—of none other than the River Liffey, no less—The Morrison has a great variation of swanky rooms, good lighting, and classy décor, you can choose from rooms or suites to stay in. Some rooms have their own private balconies. You can also have fun at the on-site bars and grill. Musicians play at certain times of the week, and Wi-Fi access is also free.

The Westbury Hotel

($331/night)

Grafton Street, Dublin 2 | 353 16791122

www.doylecollection.com/hotels/the-westbury-hotel

Situated next to the Westbury Mall, this upscale hotel boasts of airy rooms with the most majestic, soothing interiors, marble bathrooms, and heated floors to keep you comfortable. Four poster beds and free standing baths are also around—and you can enjoy cocktails and modern meals at the hotel, too. Breakfast and Wi-Fi access are available for free.

Clontarf Castle Hotel

($206/night)

Castle Ave, Dublin 3 | 353 18332321

www.clontarfcastle.ie/

If golfing and horticulture are your things, you might have a grand time staying at the Clontarf Castle Hotel has some of the most stylish rooms around—and you can choose between simple rooms, or suites, all of which are airy and classically glamorous. You can also enjoy classic Irish afternoon tea. Meeting and Wedding facilities are also available, and Wi-Fi access is around for free.

Chapter 7 Unique Dublin Experiences

Staying in Dublin would not be complete if you won't visit some unique spots, and experience adventures that you wouldn't be able to try anywhere else. While it is mostly serene, Dublin would surely make you experience amazing things, especially if you try the ones below…

Feel like a Royal at the Dublin Castle

Dame Street, Dublin 2 | 353 16458813

www.dublincastle.ie

Around for over 700 years now, visiting the Dublin Castle would allow you to stay at the Irish Seat of Power in the 13th century. Maybe, you'd be around during State Banquets or events featuring the Irish President. Visit the Drawing Room and feel like you're one of the Queen's ladies-in-waiting—and you can just go the heart of the city afterwards. It's definitely a unique experience waiting for you!

The Gaelic Game Experience

32 Claude Road, Dublin 9 | 353 12544292

www.experiencegaelicgames.com

Situated at the French Youth Rugby School, you can now experience a hands-on, on the spot training of the Gaelic Games—which includes hurling, Gaelic Football, and Gaelic Handball. If you're visiting Dublin with family and friends, this is a good way to bond with one another while literally enjoying the field. It's also a far cry from the usual serenity that Dublin exudes—and will help you appreciate the place more!

Shamrock Irish Adventures

Dublin Dublin 8 | 353 16727651

www.shamrockeradventures.com/tours/aran-rocker-tour

The shamrock is a big sign of Ireland and is als
St. Patrick's Day—and what better way to see Ir
unique manner than by participating in the Shar
Adventures? Go all around Dublin all the way to t
Islands—together with local Gaelic speakers who'd
feel like you have gone back in time! See archaeolog
remains, visit Emerald Isle, Galway City, and visit Inis Noir
while in a ferry! It's a good way to relax—and you can also rent
a bike so you can personalize the tour a bit.

Try the Wicklow Mountains Tour

Dublin, Ireland | 353 18980700

www.wicklowmountainstour.ie

The Wicklow Mountains are magnificent mountain ranges that would allow you to see Dublin—and maybe even Ireland in a brand new light. You'll go all the way to Glendalough and its lush, serene settings, and even see the Avoca Mill—one of the oldest mills not just in Dublin, but in the whole world! While there, you can also visit the Avoca Village—see and appreciate its rustic charm, and may even find new friends along the way, too.

Dublin Discovered Boat Tours

Bachelors Walk, Dublin Dublin 1 | 353 14730000

www.dublindiscovered.ie

This 45-minute boat tour will take you around the River Liffey so you can go around Dublin while in the waters. You'd be able to visit well-known sites such as the Jeanie Johnston, Ha'Penny Bridge, and Custom House, amongst others. Boats are weather-proof—so you can go whether it's summer or winter, and surely, you'd have such a relaxing time while there!

Nights of Terror Dracula Ghost Tour

18 Slievebloom Park, Dublin | 353 12548650

...etzgocitytours.com

Why not have fun trying to find ghosts while you're in the Fair City? Apparently, some people believe that there are ghosts trying to find their way in the old city of Dublin. This ghost tour would take you to Dublin's Trinity College, Christ Church, and Temple Bar, and you'd be learning about the culture and history of Dublin—courtesy of the Count and Countess! Surely, this is the only tour of its kind in Dublin—and that's why you definitely should not miss it!

Have fun at the ZipIt Forest Adventures

High Wire Adventure Centre, Tibradden Wood, Dublin | 353 51858008

www.zipit.ie/welcome-to-zipit-forest-adventures

You'll surely be able to push your boundaries while at the ZipIt Forest Adventures! Enjoy amazing tree trail challenges, a fun zipline, and be around people who also want to have good, clean fun. The staff is famous for being friendly, too.

Visit the Coolmine Equestrian Centre

Coolmine, Dublin | 353 14588447

www.coolmineequestrian.ie

Located at the Coolmine Equestrian Centre at the Dublin Foothills, an equestrian ride at the Coomine Centre would allow you to see the Irish Sea and the Leinster Capital Centre. Visit the Holiday Centre to get a taste of Irish Holidays, and check out the stables and riding school to enhance your knowledge about horses and wildlife.

Enjoy Eating at the Canal Boat Restaurant

Charlemont Place, Dublin 2 | 353 14731000

www.canalboatrestaurant.ie

If you want a different kind of eating and sightsee[ing] experience, you might as well try going to the Can[al] Restaurant where you could travel from Charlemo[nt] way to the Grand Canal while enjoying an exquisit[e] course meal. Refreshing drinks are also available for your enjoyment, as well.

1916 Rebellion Walking Tour

23 Wicklow Street, the International Bar, Dublin | 353 868583847

www.1916rising.com

Dive into the past by joining the 1916 Rebellion Tour—a testament of the Easter Rising, and a reminder of how Dublin came to be what it is now!

Chapter 8 Shopping Destinations

Shopping in Dublin is also fun. You don't have the usual malls you probably have in mind, but you'd get to enjoy creatively structured buildings that will allow you to see beautiful things while enjoying shopping, too!

Here's where you could spend your hard-earned cash.

Powerscourt Townhouse Center

59 South William Street, Dublin 2 | 353 16794144

www.powerscourtcentre.com

With a cuddly, huge bear greeting you as you arrive, the Powerscourt Townhouse Center is often deemed to be a creative space located at one of the old castles in Dublin. With its Medieval charm, you'd have more fun shopping at various jewelry, clothes, and fashion stores while in the area! You'd also be able to sample Dublin's history with the help of daily guided tours that you can avail of. You might also want to visit the on-site doll store and the Irish Dancing Museum. Internet kiosks are also around, but Wi-Fi access is free of charge.

St. Stephen's Green Shopping Center

Stephens Green, Dublin 2 | 353 14780888

www.stephensgreen.com

After visiting St. Stephen's Gardens, make sure to set foot at this incredible three-story shopping center that houses some of the best restaurants and shops in all of Dublin! It's a good place to buy those souvenirs—and sample what Dublin has to offer.

The Hazel House

Mutton Lane, Dublin 16 | 353 868701692

www.thehazelhouse.ie/store/c1/Featured_Products.html

One of Dublin's best kept secrets, this hole-in-the-wall store offers products created by Dublin's very own artisans. But not only would you find the best handicrafts, visiting the Hazel House would also allow you to join crafting classes, and pet and feed the animals at the in-house farm. This certainly is the perfect place to buy gifts and unforgettable items you could bring home with you.

Books Upstairs

17 D'Olier Street, Dublin | 353 16778566

www.facebook.com/Books-Upstairs-249287641781861

If you're a bibliophile, you would surely appreciate Books Upstairs—a carefully stocked bookstore in Dublin! Designed to look like one of those old time bookstores, you'd feel a sense of peace while here. Not only will you be able to buy books, you'd also have the chance to join poetry sessions at the store's very own Library Café, and you'd also be able to join book discussions, interviews, and book launches, as well.

Kevin and Howlin

31 Nassau Street, Dublin | www.kevinandhowlin.com

If you love Tweed, you'd appreciate Kevin and Howlin for the sell some of the most incredible and impeccable tweed clothing around—not just in Dublin, but in the whole world, too.

Lucy's Lounge

11 Fownses Street, Temple Bar, Dublin 2 | 353 16774779

www.lucysloungevintage.com

Around since 1987, this is one of the best Vintage stores in all of Ireland! With some of the most beautiful and charming dressing rooms, have fun checking out hand-picked garments that have that special, old-time charm in them—but could work in the modern world, too! They also have their own designs—crafted from scraps of old clothes in the aptly named *Lucy's Lab*.

Sheridan's

11 South Anne Street, Dublin | www.sheridanscheesemongers.com

A world-famous cheese shop, you definitely have to visit this gourmet store—buy the cheeses you want, and have a chance to taste them first, too.

Cow's Lane Designer Studio

2 Pudding Row, Dublin 8 | 353 15240001

www.cowslanedesignerstudio.ie

Boasting of some of Dublin's local designers' best creations, Cow's Lane Designer Studio features a vast range of clothes, accessories, shoes that are all creatively designed in Dublin. Surely, you'd have items that no one else in your hometown has!

Avoca Handweavers

11-13 Suffolk Street, Dublin | 353 16774215

www.avoca.com/

At the old town of Avoca lies the best handcrafted items in all of Dublin. After shopping, you can go and eat their famous fishcakes, too!

Chapter 9 Nightlife in Dublin

Have a taste of what Dublin has to offer at night out its famous party spots.

The Brazen Head

20 Bridge St, Dublin | 353 16779549

www.brazenhead.com

With a gothic medieval feel, you surely should not miss what is known as Dublin's oldest pub! Having been around since 1198, a visit would allow you to experience what pubs really are about. With live music every night, enjoy Guinness Beer together with your choice of food! Favorites include Clonakilty Black Pudding Salad, Pork Cutlet Provencal, Smoked Salmon, Greek Salad, Glazed Loin of Bacon, and Lemon & Garlic Chicken among others. Vegetarian meals are available, as well.

Merry Ploughboy Irish Music Pub

Edsmontown Road, Rockbrook Dublin, Dublin 16 | 353 14931495

www.mpbpub.com/show-tradtional-music-dublin.php

At 8 each night, you can enjoy live, traditional Irish Music by visiting the Merry Ploughboy Irish Pub. Not only will you get to catch bands sing live, you can join the fun by singing and dancing, as well. And of course, go try an unforgettable dinner consisting of homemade seafood chowder, shank of lamb, root vegetable soup, Irish angus beef, free range Limerick Chicken, and apple pie, amongst other! You'd surely have a merry good time while here!

O'Donoghue's Bar

15 Merrion Row, Dublin 2 | 353 16607194

www.odonoghues.ie

.d to be the one of the most talked-about pubs in Dublin, O Donoghue's injects a modern twist to the rustic charm of most Irish pubs and attractions. With traditional music, violin shows, and local art on the walls, you would definitely have an authentic Dubliner experience while here. Guest Rooms are also available for you to stay in, should you choose to go that route.

The Long Haul

51 S Great Georges Street, Dublin 2 | 353 14751590

Around since the Victorian Era, this hole-in-the-wall pub has a warm ambience and houses a collection of antique mirrors and clocks—together with gin and whiskey that don't taste like what you have at home. Stopping by surely would grant you a treat!

Mulligan's

Poolbeg St, Dublin 2 | 353 16775582

You'd surely enjoy your pints of beer while at this celebrated pub! Aside from Jameson's and Guinness, there are other types of beer and wine that you might enjoy here. It's such a good place for a nightout—and for spending time with family and friends.

The Palace

21 Fleet Street, Dublin 2 | 353 16717388

www.thepalacebardublin.com

Often part of traditional Irish pub crawls, The Palace has been around since 1823—giving it that authentic, medieval charm that you're looking for in a pub! Aside from having amazing drinks, you'd also get the chance to buy The Palace pints—a rare collectible that your family and friends would surely be in awe of.

Porter House Dublin

16-18 Parliament St 2, Dublin | 353 16798847

www.theporterhouse.ie

The Porter House has been brewing craft beer since 1996. While modern by some standards, you can still experience an authentic pub feeling here. They have beer, stout, ales, and lagers of every kind—with some beverages available for special occasions, too.

Vicar Street

58-59 Thomas Street, Dublin | 353 14546656

www.vicarstreet.ie

With some of the most memorable shows you'll ever get to see in your life, you definitely should not miss the chance to visit the lively and bright Vicar Street! With musicians playing beautiful songs, you'd also get to learn about their history—such as the *Simon and Garfunkel story*! You could rent the place for personal celebrations and events, and learn more about Dublin by visiting their in-house gallery.

Stag's Head

1 Dame Court, off Dame Street, Dublin 2 | 353 16713701

www.louisfitzgerald.com/stagshead

A pub full of history and glory, Stag's Head should definitely be on your nighttime list! With old world charm, granite tabletops, and marble floors, there's a certain kind of luxury that you'd feel while here. Tuesdays are folksy, ukulele nights—so you can enjoy the music, and while there, make sure to check out their breaded brie cheese, chicken coujons, and cocktail sausages, among others.

Chapter 10 Safety Tips and Survival Guide

Make sure that your trip isn't just unforgettable—but that it is also safe by keeping these safety tips in mind.

Safety and Precaution/ Customs/ Etiquette

1. Before arriving in Dublin, take note that you are allowed to bring the following—but only if you are from other EU Countries: 10 liters of spirits, 200 cigars, 3200 cigarettes, 250 mls of Eeu de toilette, 60 mls of perfume, 20 liters of fortified wine, and at least 180 euros of dutiable goods.

2. When in pubs or busy streets, always keep an eye on your belongings as pick-pocketing and bag snatching are not uncommon.

3. When staying in hostels, take note that drug selling/pushing in some streets could be prevalent. Make sure to keep an eye on your surroundings, and don't trust just about anyone you meet.

4. If using a rental car, make sure to park it only at secure car parks.

5. If using a bicycle, make sure to lock both wheels when it is not in use.

6. Do not wander around areas you are unfamiliar with, especially if you are alone. Don't act as if you don't know where you're going. Don't act "lost".

7. Most currency exchange counters and banks are at the Dublin International Airport. ATMs are liberally spread around the city, especially in most shopping destinations.

8. Take note that smoking is banned in all workspaces—even in pubs. If you want to smoke, do it in your hotel room—make sure it is smoking. Otherwise, you might have to pay a fine.

9. Never interrupt Irish storytellers—it is deemed unethical.

10. Do not take jokes too seriously. Learn to take things with a grain of salt.

11. As much as you can, avoid political or religious discussions—just to be on the safe side of things.

12. It is not usual to tip taxi drivers—but make sure to thank them and express gratitude for their work. Thank bus drivers who help you in and out of the bus, as well.

13. As for restaurants, it would be good to tip at least 10 cents—but you do not have to do the same at bars and pubs. If in case an Irish family invites you to eat with them, make sure to wait until all of them have found their place in the table before you start eating. Try to eat everything on your plate as it is deemed disrespectful if you don't. Be ready for these may be generous portions. To say you're finished, simply put the fork and knife parallel to each other on the plate's right side—but try to leave room for those delectable desserts!

14. There are no major health concerns in the area—which is good for you!

15. For more tourist information, try to visit the Dublin Tourism Office. It is located at the former site of St. Andrew's Church on Suffolk Street. Visit their website at www.visitdublin.com.

Emergency Numbers

Here are emergency numbers you should always keep in your backpocket—or your phone, whichever works!

Emergency Ambulance, Firemen, Police

999 or 112

When calling, make sure to provide what exactly is going on, and the landmark near where you're making the call—or where the emergency is. Make sure to be as detailed as possible, especially when describing the incident.

Hospitals

Rotunda Hospital, Parnell Street, Dublin 1 | 353 18730700

Beaumont Hospital, Beaumont Rd, Dublin 9 | 353 18093000

Vehicle Breakdowns

Automobile Association (AA) Breakdown Service | 1800 667788

www.aaireland.ie

Take note that if you're going to need their services, you have to pay an annual fee of €220.

Roadside Assistance

Royal Automobile Club Breakdown Help | 44 8448913111

For roadside accidents or emergencies, make sure to get in touch with them.

Victim Support

Irish Tourist Assistance Service (ITAS) | 1890 365 700 | 353 16610562

info@itas.ie

6-7 Hanover Street East, Dublin 2

Mon to Sat 10AM to 6PM | Sundays and Holidays 12PM to 6PM

In the unfortunate event that you become the victim of a crime while in Dublin—or anywhere in Ireland, it's best that you call ITAS so utmost assistance could be given to you. Their staff is able to speak lots of languages, so you could easily get help and understanding. Tourist Offices everywhere in the country also offer information about ITAS, as well.

Keep these tips and numbers in mind and you'd surely have a great time while in Dublin! Enjoy!

Conclusion

Once again thank you for choosing *Lost Travelers*!

I hope this book was able to provide you with the best travel tips when visiting Dublin.

And we hope you enjoy your travels.

"Travel Brings Power And Love Back To Your Life"

- Rumi

Finally, if you enjoyed this book, then I'd like to ask you for a favor, would you be kind enough to leave a review for this book on Amazon? It'd be greatly appreciated!

> Simply search the keywords "Dublin Lost Travelers" on Amazon or go to our Author page "Lost Travelers" to review.

Your satisfaction is important to us! If you were not happy with the book please email us with the title, your comment and suggestion so we may consider any improvements and serve you better in the next edition.

> Email: SevenTreeImprove@gmail.com

Thank you and good luck!

NOTES

NOTES

NOTES

NOTES

Preview Of 'Vienna: The Ultimate Vienna Travel Guide By A Traveler For A Traveler

What comes to mind when you hear the mention of Vienna? Is it the world's famous coffee houses, its famous heuriger or do you think of neighborhoods that are almost a millennia old? If you know a little bit about the city, you probably understand that it is the capital of Austria and the largest of the nine states of Austria housing nearly a third of Austria's entire population.

What you don't know is that it is the 6th largest city by population within the city limits in the EU and was once (in the early 20th century) the largest German-speaking city in the world before the split of Austro-Hungarian Empire during World War 1 when the city had about 2 million residents. It now hosts the 2nd largest number of German speakers after Berlin and is home to OPEC and UN. It has also been ranked as one of the most livable cities in the world several times according to the Quality of Life Survey, the most prosperous city in the world according to the UN-Habitat and one of the best in terms of culture of innovation and a lot more. Do you also know that it receives well over 3 million tourists every single year? Well, if the Baroque castles, gardens and the famous 19th century Ringstrasse lined with park, monuments, and grand buildings is anything to go by, I'd visit this wonderful city as often as possible.

Vienna, famously referred to as the city of music and the city of dreams, is undoubtedly one of those places you'd want to visit before you die. With a rich history going back to the 1st century AD, you can bet that it has seen a lot throughout its years of existence. This coupled with its strategic geographical location near Czech Republic, Slovakia and Hungary, it is certain that it plays an important role both as a political, economic and cultural center. Besides, its historic center has been designated a UNESCO World Heritage Site making it even more attractive to the world over.

If you are planning to visit Vienna, let this book be your guide to make your visit truly worthwhile. We will take a journey through the pages of history as we move to the present then narrow it down to the top places to visit, museums, art galleries and a lot more.

Check out the rest of Vienna: The Ultimate Vienna Travel Guide on Amazon by simply searching it.

Check Out Our Other Books

Below you'll find some of our other popular books that are on Amazon and Kindle as well. Simply search the titles below to check them out. Alternatively, you can visit our author page (Lost Travelers) on Amazon to see other work done by us.

- Vienna: The Ultimate Vienna Travel Guide By A Traveler For A Traveler

- Barcelona: The Ultimate Barcelona Travel Guide By A Traveler For A Traveler

- London: The Ultimate London Travel Guide By A Traveler For A Traveler

- Istanbul: The Ultimate Istanbul Travel Guide By A Traveler For A Traveler

- Vietnam: The Ultimate Vietnam Travel Guide By A Traveler For A Traveler

- Peru: The Ultimate Peru Travel Guide By A Traveler For A Traveler

- Australia: The Ultimate Australia Guide By A Traveler For A Traveler

- Japan: The Ultimate Japan Travel Guide By A Traveler For A Traveler

- New Zealand: The Ultimate New Zealand Travel Guide By A Traveler For A Traveler

- Dublin: The Ultimate Dublin Travel Guide By A Traveler For A Traveler

- Thailand: The Ultimate Thailand Travel Guide By A Traveler For A Traveler

- Iceland: The Ultimate Iceland Travel Guide By A Traveler For A Traveler

- Santorini: The Ultimate Santorini Travel Guide By A Traveler For A Traveler

- Italy: The Ultimate Italy Travel Guide By A Traveler For A Traveler

You can simply search for these titles on the Amazon website to find them.

Printed in Great Britain
by Amazon